Long Alabama Summer

poems by

Katherine D. Perry

Finishing Line Press
Georgetown, Kentucky

Long Alabama Summer

for Charles, Zi, and Nate
who get me up every morning and put me to bed every night

and for the Alabama Gulf Coast
that shaped me

ACKNOWLEDGMENTS

With thanks to the editors of the following publications in which these poems
(sometimes in altered versions and with different titles) originally appeared:

13th Moon, For Addie Mae
Bloodroot Literary Magazine, Chasing Julia Strudwick Tutwiler
Eco-Chick, water like form
Dead Mule of Southern Literature, Storm Wake and Early Summer Babysitter
Melusine, of Woman in the 21st Century, Beach Girls
Poetry Quarterly, Unload
RiverSedge, Emiko's Needle
Sleet Magazine, Finding Legs
Sojourn, Daddy Gave Me Away and A Pauper's Art
Southern Women's Review, caverns
The Auburn Circle, Ningyo and Sunday 11:15 am
Women's Studies, Playing Gender

Publisher: Leah Maines

Editor: Christen Kincaid

Cover Art: MaryEtta Perry

Author Photo: Kathryn Brannon

Cover Design: Elizabeth Maines McCleavy

Printed in the USA on acid-free paper.
Order online: www.finishinglinepress.com
　　　　　also available on amazon.com

Author inquiries and mail orders:
Finishing Line Press
P. O. Box 1626
Georgetown, Kentucky 40324
U. S. A.

Table of Contents

Introduction

May

June

July

August

September

Introduction

My first poetic love affair, where I read every poem she had written and her biographies and slept with her books as my pillows, was with Sylvia Plath. I adored the Moderns, the Imagists, and the Beats, but Plath moved me from beyond the grave even when I was too young to really understand love affairs.

Plath taught me to use my life, to be brave enough to confess, but she also showed me that the truth is irrelevant. Many of these poems are confessional. Many more of them seem more confessional than they are. I did grow up in Alabama. However, what is truth and what is fiction is never clear, sometimes (or maybe especially) to even the author. As I age, I find the relationship between memory and history instructional and complicated.

I have had many love affairs since Plath, as we all do when we grow and move through the world. But those early loves, the ones that opened doors and imprinted themselves on us, shape much of this collection. Thank you for meeting me here and there.

May

And the field daisy eyes
Of black and white black white black people
And I'm gonna put white hands
And black hands and brown and yellow hands
And red clay earth hands in it
Touching everybody with kind fingers

~Langston Hughes, "Daybreak in Alabama"

Early Summer Babysitter

My feet swing over my parent's garden;
he pushes me from behind, his long hands
on my favorite superman t-shirt.
Under my toes run rows of corn, strawberries, squash;
my nail-bitten hands grip the black nylon rope
holding a round wooden seat to the live oak tree.
He's sixteen so he talks about television shows,
and I'm six so I pretend to know them all.
Between our chatter, the world flies past
in blurs of bark, falling green leaves, white sky.
I want to stop, put my feet onto brown soil,
make sure that summer air bakes
this memory into ashes.

Mom told him that I like to swing
so he stands in tall summer grass and pushes me
over gardens—over okra and snap beans
and I lie to him about what I know, what I like,
and he smiles when he pretends to enjoy me.
We have all day to kill, and we don't know
each other well enough to know the difference;
I smile and giggle like I've been taught to do
when the swing makes me fly into clouds.
He asks if I want to go higher; I say yes
meaning no, meaning I've had enough;
I know that nothing edible grows in air.

He mentions *One Day at a Time* and a girl named Valerie,
and I look over to the neighbor's barn, to hay bales
stacked neatly inside; their softness spoiled
by fingers prodding. I wish I could make
a single leap from swing to loft or air
or could speed past him and into the garden.
I want to run down rows of corn, leaves
of towering stalks slapping my face;
I want to hide myself in camouflage
of silk tassels and ears that forgive my forming screams.

Storm Wake

Resting in the eye of Frederic, 1979,
I listened to the stillness, the silent groans
of live oak trees hammered by insane air and water.
I soaked up the calm of a once dangerous house,
now quiet, now sleeping.

Sky reappeared; the stars remained unaffected.
But as I looked up, I knew all would be changed
when sunlight showed me the source of the pelting
pine-sap smell, the fresh scent of twisted trunks,
and unearthed roots.

The eye passed.
Wind ripped shingles
like hair from a scalp; rain seeped
under every door and towel stuffed
to keep it out. I lost the sky, my bearings,
all sense of a safe world. Windows cracked
like jawbones; fences crumbled into heaps
of mangled flesh in another woman's garden.

Wind howled like a madman; his fingers
pushed over fort, sandbox, and oak tree swing.
He battered cars, mailboxes, and satellite
dishes. When his anger finally passed over,
the sun crept out again, somewhat timid.

Morning showed me my coastal town, and I,
unwilling to acknowledge the terror,
grabbed up the chainsaw, and cleared away the evidence.
It was like pouring makeup on a bruise.
I thought I could make it okay.
I thought no one would notice.

Uncorking Bottles: Writing Sonnets

Unless I can build a new set of shelves
in basements long since visited, I guess
my travels must wind into myself, delve
into dim, walled-off spaces to confess
in metaphorical mirrors that hang
in imagined hallways those obvious
liquids, those hidden emotions, that sprang
from the child me. Underneath the callous,
behind every cork, a perfected wine,
aged and protected from light, lips, and air,
awaits me. So, I go down, un-shelf my
precious bottles and settle in a chair

to drink. Not like there is no tomorrow
but like tonight is all that matters now.

Lost Photo of Junior Prom

Not seventeen, she chooses to wear white
taffeta handed down from previous
dances, wraps a daring purple ribbon,
matched gloves to transform it to her budding
tastes. She clings to a tall, thin, young man who
spends months showing her what it means to come

home to howling parents (they believed her
to be Alabama trash) because she
spends delicate hours and hours letting him
wrap himself inside her every layer,
like she can save him the way his father
saves gunshot victims in crowded ERs.

In this photograph, she looks like this night
might match every fairytale she has dreamed.

History, rewritten

Summer lives in coarse buzzes
of threatening horseflies.
Impotent breezes hiss through
green pine needles, and acrid
smells of chlorine-shocked water
weave into bitter sharp fumes
of new plastic rafts that float
on mini-tidal-waves
churned up by the frantic splashes
of uninvited cousins,
their hiccupped laughter bleeding
into the released spring coil
of a dive   board   vacated.

To forget, I lay out blue-print
ideas: crisp, clean pages
that outline long flat walkways,
pools of smooth salt water
ponds, even cleverly hidden cupboards
for storing cushions to protect delicate skin
from our sun-heated lounge chairs.
As if   I might be able
to construct something solid
on these teetering foundations.
As if   the buzzing could stop.

Nature Trails

Older kids drink and smoke;
we hide in wood-paneled corners,
clinging to each other's newly shaved skin.
To escape, we dare to leave
crowded parties to be alone: let go and play
adult roles in the stories we want to live.

I put my fingers in your hand,
lead you to trails I had run
and biked throughout most of my childhood,
rein in my pace from skip to the unsophisticated swagger
I see on adults.
Without flashlights or streetlamps,
we grope our way past the last fork:
far enough from civilization to openly kiss
before we crawl beyond
short-needle pines as they attempt to grow
vertical again after hurricane Frederic.

Because it feels good, I keep going.
But in moonless dark,
I search your eyes for signs of fear;
I can't be sure if markers point me the right way.
When we reach the terminus,
no landmark or waterfall,
I look away from you; we walk back
trying to pretend we never traveled there,
trying to understand why we should feel guilty
for what seems joyous continuations of every explorers dream: to go boldly.

I return there by daylight,
look for small patches of ground
where we turned left or back, look for
stains or footprints that never existed.
Instead, I find only my own
amazement at ordinary shapes
of dogwoods that loomed magically

and listen to silence that screamed
with wildlife when we explored it at midnight
in the sticky summer heat of our early teens.

A Pauper's Art

She had nothing, but had it all
bottled up in colored glass
on shelves that lined the walls
of her childhood room. Last

year she uncorked each glass color
and discovered—in blue—music dancing
in the childhood room. But her mother
crushed it when her father's raving

refused a piano, and music stilled.
Later—in yellow—the child found oil
raving thick on canvas and willed
her hand to move steady and loyal,

to lift yellow sunrises from clarity.
The globs of aging oil smirked,
rebelled. The stubborn canvas held steady
against her premature forms and shucked

her attempts. But aging colored glass
whispered to her while she slept,
the growing forms inside held fast,
the colors—impatient—leapt

from whispers to fingers
to find pencil and paper.
Words—in red—leap and linger
on sheets hidden between layers

of mattresses. She steals paper
from parents or school without
notice, she hides it and her labor
because it holds—in silence—the shouts

of a girl, whose parents could not
afford a piano or oils or lessons,

whose walls, lined with singing bottles,
held nothing, but opened to it all.

Wind Release

Children who spend early years on the Gulf
understand differently the cycles of the moon.
They notice humans bending to the same will
that the earth follows, the water in their bodies
shifting from waxing to waning
or from waning to waxing.
They understand that moods, like waves,
erode the things they brush against,
and they figure out, too early,
to let them pass over without putting up a fight.

Children who spend early years on the Gulf
also know about the power of wind;
not the quick tempered tornados that plague
the center of the country, or the sustained blowing
that arrives on the two oceanic coasts,
but a breeze that relieves the August heat
and the occasional hurricane force
that at least the birds warn against
giving everyone a slim chance to survive.

June

Here, where the water darkens, red,
where we sift the earth for sherds,
I wash an arrowhead
into the sun's steel-white gleam,

then sieve fists of rock through my hands
till I finger something strange—
a tiny ball of polished iron,
shot-metal distilled from clay.

~Jake Adam York, "On Tallasseehatchee Creek"

Sarah Discovers Stories

She pulls the strings tight. In one knot, a thread
can weave shield and sword; her mindful care
cradles her unformed foot, lines, dread.
She works years to fight what she's left unsaid,
her quilt lengthens, fingers ache, but she dares
to pull the strings to tighter knots. Threads
carry colors, histories, and legions of dead:
insignias and antiquated scripts: snares
to hold her, formed in foot and line. Dread
wraps her in fabrics of lies she created,
sweeps away scraps she cannot wear.
She pulls a drawstring tight, loops the knot, threads
the remainder of unused yarn around the spool head
and turns finally to an artificial prayer:
rid me of my deforming foot. Lines pull dread,
and when Sarah darns her socks in patterned reds,
she curls her back hard against the wooden chair,
pulls the string tight. In its knot, the thread
will hold her forming foot, her line, her dread.

Residue

once, in a campground bathroom
my best friend saw bruises,
        shoulders and biceps
        purple and blue;
in her eyes
        fear and shock
like when he put the cigarette out
on the back of his hand.

desperate to touch him
we played *rough* in the yard:
his fists better than loneliness.

I slept with my colors
wrapped tightly in long sleeved
pajamas, punched him when he
would not kiss me, covered him
in my arms trying to feel the life
I deadened in pleasant doses
of toxic chemicals.

when I finally came clean,
said it to him in a haze of smoke,
he looked as if he did not know me,
        arteries and valves
        red and orange
in my chest cavity
        constricting in silence
like when the man who left bruises
jumped in the car with another woman,
drove away without a glance:
        leaving a residue
        like a cigarette burn,
        like a punch to the jaw.

Ningyou[i]

Sometimes
when we make
thunder at midnight
with his grunting body
pushing in waves,
I question this wifehood:
clean the porcelain,
pour the tea.

Like koi in the tiny pool
surrounded by pruned
green gardens,
I swim circles
to lay eggs,
offer my flesh
for sushi.
Submerged,
yearning for air,
I watch him on land:
work his day,
stop for *sake*
where bar-girls praise
his manhood,
giggle at puns,
pour beer before he needs,
leave me only red-faced
leftovers.

I warm his bath, feed his daughter,
keep her perfect, a doll
for his eyes.
But she is my dream,
my flight from this water;
I wait for the day
she soars away from this closing pond
and laughs at me
still swimming.

Having Children

For years, I read poems using children as metaphors
for poetry. Men, mainly, "giving birth" to their words
and tending their lines like changing diapers.
Even when I was childless, I could not square
this comparison with my own poetry writing.
They do not love me,
do not need me,
do not cry in the night.

For years, men taught me poetry writing:
some fathers, some not. In classrooms, in libraries,
in homes I should have never entered, I listened to them
explain their visions for the structures of stanzas,
for the taxonomies of devices, for the methodological
ways into the enchantment of creation.
They did not hear me,
did not read me,
did not bother to understand that my way was different.

Now I spend my years preparing, washing, helping to build
children's minds. I find moments for myself,
like the ones required for writing poems, more and more fleeting.
I balance my life against the lives of my offspring.
They breathe my air,
hum my songs,
speak my words.

My daughter sleeps in her crib;
my body builds my son,
and I turn to scratch out
ideas that come from places I cannot explain.

Creation is the closest thing I know to magic,
but a poem is not a child.

Beach Girls

after a 1920's photo

On that white sand
your white skin
needs imitation Japanese
parasols to keep you that shade.

Behind you, other white women
stick their toes in the Gulf
of Mexico, and nowhere in sight
does anyone of color appear;
and this is Mississippi, after all.
Instead, your rolled American
flag, your stylish one-piece bathing suits,
and your finger wave hair
are the only (now grey) colors
in this photograph.

I cannot help but ask,   who
cleaned your homes,   who
washed those delicate clothes, who
made your packed lunches.

Nowhere can I find those workers.
It is 1920, remember,
and we could not vote either.

Emiko's Needle

I wonder what Emiko does, what she chose
when options landed on her stone porch
like headlines of a tossed newspaper.
I imagine a husband's booming voice
demanding his orange juice in a cleaner glass
and her bedroom, too small for a sewing table,
big enough for her knees to fall open.
Her hair falls the length of her back
when he isn't home to pull it in his fists.
I imagine her reflection in the mirror
showing hints of caverns the wind and rain
make of our bodies, of the smiles we fake.
Maybe she smiles at herself to confirm
that mountains can be climbed,
that outside her walls, a sun rises.
She bows her head to her past,
to the mountain before her, to the light.

When children cry, she soothes them;
her stone feet huddle in the bottom of a bag
she was not allowed to make.
Her needle moves swiftly into her son's socks,
her daughter's bib, her husband's button.
She mends, never creates
the lush gowns and jackets
she once made for me.
She rarely remembers she can.
Colors of thread blow through her mind
like flags of countries she will never
again leave Japan to see.
Between her legs she holds a pillow
so that her knees don't bump in her sleep.
Between the frame of her home and the frame
of her bones, she slips into wind and thunder.

Sunday, 11:15am

For we are consumed by thine anger
and by thy wrath are we troubled.
Thou has set our iniquities before thee,
Our secret sins in the light of thy countenance.
Psalms 90:7-8

I've outgrown this.
The glass leaves spots
on my skin like a disease.

I watch the crystal prisms
dangling on chandeliers
like I did as a child,
stuck behind the too-tall pulpit
reciting names: Genesis to Revelations,
correctly and in order.
I spouted ancient language,
watched the lights, and wished to sit.

Later, squirming in the pew,
wanting to laugh and play,
I was told to sit still:
not to smile. I watched the coffin,
thinking of the dead girl I hated,
and when she passed me,
I caught my face in the box's surface.

The last time I was here,
I marched determined to the altar
costumed in white and plastic pearls
that caught the candle's flickers
and sprinkled them across my face.
Strange that I remember *that*,
not the minister's words,
just the dots of light covering my body.

I came back today
to figure out what I lost then.

But I just watch the stained glass:
the colors on my skin.
They fascinate me.

Daddy Gave Me Away

over an all-you-can-eat
buffet, a Gravely lawn mower
my only dowry.

So I moved from daddy's home
to his shiny new kitchen,
where I learned to cook
country fried steak
for a husband's fattening stomach
and washed dirty work
uniforms to kill the smell
of grease and soured sweat.

I learned the recipes
by heart at first, and then
gradually learned to dash
in spices for interest,
praying for a secret ingredient,
for some perfect seasoning
to make the deal my daddy made
work, to make my life bearable.

At 17, I knew nothing of the trade,
but time and heat gave rise
to a woman, and she left him,
his kitchen, stomach, mower,
and daddy too.

No daddy, I'm not through,
If God made man from dust,
I can do better.

July

now as i move, mouth quivering with silks
my skin runs soft with eyes.
descending into my legs, i follow obscure birds
purchasing orthopedic wings.
the air is late this summer.

~Sonia Sanchez, "under a soprano sky"

History of a Haircut

I'm going under; my neck stretched, my head
pushed down by Della into the soapy warm
water. She massages my tired scalp to red

then orders me to her chair between swarms
of workers dancing around caped clients
like Sunday mornings where I learned alarming

numbers of stories that still chase me defiantly
even when I think I've finally lost them. Today,
I remember Delilah and Samson and his reliance

on hair for strength. Della pulls up the frayed
ends of my overgrown, neglected bob, clicks
her tongue, digs out her clips, and combs her way

into a neatly segregated nest. Her fingers mimic
a new hair line as she cuts my precious power,
and I wonder how long it will be before her tricks

will have me tied in thick ropes; how long till I'll cower
under the temple, pray for mercy and vengeance,
travel up, up, up, out of this punishment and devour

the betrayal with broken walls. By chance,
Della catches me in the mirror, sees my troubled look
and smiles, one woman to another, grants

me assurance of her innocence.
                                      What took
years to learn, takes even longer to undo:
we're not harlots, thieves, or crooks.

Delilah, Della, and I get haircuts too.
We maneuver the aisles; then we grow (out) new.

Apprentice

Beneath her, I curl myself into a quiet knot,
watch her work in fits of mania. Her quick,
meticulous hands dig perfect stitches;
my fingers scramble to mimic her methods,
remember her rhythm.

Beneath her, scraps of fabric dance
like axed chickens. My hands reach
across splintered wood floors to the cotton debris.
I steal these fragments for my own quilt box,
run my fingers up the flower prints. Down feathers
cradle my head as she works through the night,
her eyes puffed and bloody, her needle furious
to finish the final pieces.

Beneath her, I tremble. Shards meld together,
become something I can never guess.
In the belly of the blanket, my face blends into
swatches of color, into shapes I cannot see.
She lays the blanket over me, over the table over me,
smoothes the wrinkles of us both.
As light peeks through morning,
I fall into comfortable sleep.

Beneath the place where she once stood, I dream
I stand. Wind blows like her breath,
like my breath over a quilted flower fabric.
Her arms wrap around me, move me in her steps.
Our fingers dance the rhythm of loops,
follow the beat of well-learned stitches.

When I wake, I move into the empty space,
open the rainbow box of gathered color,
begin my own appliqué pattern.
I follow the beat of well-learned stitches;
my hands use her hands to loop in rhythms.

A Portrait of Elly

Even amidst fierce flames the golden lotus can be planted[ii]

Maybe a touch of peach would help,

a color to bring her to life.

I try blue in her eyes,

maybe some red on her lips

or a smaller brush to get the stroke right,

I'll bring her to life, here beside me,

her eyes becoming someone I know,

her mouth smiling like a friend,

of a girl a mother loves.

Maybe some white on her teeth,

right there...no...that's not it,

that changed her whole...face...

maybe this is more like her,

closer to a real person.

I'd leave her this way,

but this twisted smile

might hurt my fee.

Better to copy the photograph,

Alone in a bath tub

water steaming the mirror

razors slicing your shins,

A quick note to mom,

tea glass of water, bottle of pills

squeeze into the crevice

a pill, a sip, pill, sip

take a nap

let it go.

But they find you,

nurse you back to life

try to shock the hell out of you,

make you well,

but even insulin's temporary.

Another note,

milk by their bedsides,

turn on the gas,

towels and tape will hold it in.

Let her mother remember that face.

You need the rest.

The woman is perfected.

For Addie Mae

*Have you heard the one about
the shivering lives,
the never to be borne daughters and sons*
—Lucille Clifton, "Alabama 9/15/63"

I thought to name a daughter after you,
to throw all tradition to the wind and pay
tribute to what was lost: a white child
with the name of a brown girl killed six years
before I was born. A few letters strung
together as a token gesture, to say:
we are not all that way.

I too was born in Alabama, but in 1969,
and into a white, working-class family that still
bought segregation, into tradition that spit
at Malcolm, into a region that could not see
King's dream. Years have passed since
you and three other little girls
have been gone, and who remembers?

I thought to name my daughter after you,
to offer a name to the universe as a signal,
as a way to remind us how far we might
travel in only a few years.
But, you see, I have no daughter
and none on the way. There are too many
bombs in churches, men dragging men
behind trucks, obscenities carved into
car hoods to bring a child here.

I thought to name myself fearless.
I thought to stand up shouting.
I think of your sweet round face hidden under bricks and dust.
There must be something that I can offer.
There must be some way to mend.

Finding Legs

My signature danced like water in my eyes. Somehow, my flimsy body,
shaking like a red maple leaf, made it from limb to ground
without cracking, without crumbling
and the arms of the wheelchair clung strange, like they knew
I was numb, like my torso would wake at any moment and fall forward.

A nurse came and took my purse, took Chapstick from my pocket,
then the pen from my hand before taking the belt from my loops
and led me to a room where I could shut the door and cry alone.

A moment of grace
between horrors of dreams and new life:
between bark and concrete, light wind moving me down:
awake on a bed I hoped never to feel again: sheet I hoped to forget.

A moment of grace:
my tingling body, coming to   the way a foot will
when circulation has been stopped   the way a flower falls when the heat starts

Coming to
        I thought:
                coming   to consciousness
                              to reckoning
                              to blows
        with myself, with a wall

and in a sterile room, in a foreign place where underpaid nurses jostle me harshly

A moment of grace:
I run my fingers down those waking legs that could be mine,
that could move again.

Water like form

I think of it like a river swelling, like banks overtaken by day after day of downpours on saturated earth and streets covered in water that overwrought sewer systems cannot process; every feeder creek bulges so that when all of the topsoil, forgotten appliances, dead squirrels, maple leaves, human excrement, single leather shoes, and other lost relics that this never-ending storm gathers and pushes into the Mississippi, the Nile, the Thames, the Amazon, the Yangtze, I abandon my make-shift raft, crawl with my fingers and toes digging into the grasses of steep land and find refuge in a spot close enough to watch the muddy mess overtake what had been a neat and predictable river bed; as the historic layers of human records fall into corrosive water, I am struck by the leveling power, not just the reduction of our houses and beloved marble sculptures, but of the mountain making way for new elephant paths, the nest of an eagle breaking against a lowly pink tricycle, the 10-pound book moving along with the plastic grocery bag and the raccoon treading water. Suddenly, something breaks (or catches), and the river splits itself in two. We who witness will not be able to recall the exact water level when the change happened, or the precise curve of the shoreline before the flood, and we certainly will not remember the specific meteorological rhythms that cracked open our understanding of the way things worked before the swelling occurred; even the eye-witness testimonies will be thrown out because the shift, the radical realignment of the water to land, will rename even the rivers themselves. No one will even want to recall how the system once worked; I watch the floating bodies rushing past me in the water and wonder momentarily about what might be underneath the surface. Unable to answer, I climb the bank of this newly forming creature. I face a new direction.

Pantomime Assassin: March 30, 1981

During sixth-grade year, hormones bubbled,
and I squeezed myself between wooden desk, new haircut,
and brand-named denim. As I twisted round
to throw off a wandering hand from my bra strap,

a messenger knocked: *The president has been shot; Reagan is shot!*
My boyfriend, John, sidled over to me,
clamping his palm on my forearm, asking with a smile
and forced-caring: *Are you okay?*
Yes. My thoughts cartwheeled over his fingers
on my skin, and my stomach jackknifed. But I smiled.
I had learned, like Foster in *Taxi Driver*, how to belong to a man.
I knew how to never need a thing, how to perform satisfaction.

Someone wheeled in a television cart; we watched their story.
He loved her.
He wrote to her: *I would abandon*
                         the idea of getting Reagan in a second
                         if I could only win your heart
                         and live out the rest of my life with you.
Hinkley just wanted Foster's attention.
                              And there came a splitting in my head.
I was plagued with John's fake concern,
with Jeff, Lamar, and Derrick on the bus
with their hands, palms up, in seats to grab
our bodies for the thrill,
with Mike and Jim at the skating rink,
harassing for one kiss, one touch, just one…

This is obsession's outcome.

It would repeat day after day:
the pantomime of grabbing
                and pulling away.
                I never escaped the carousel horse. Up and Down.

I felt in my brain, not the funeral, but the rip made by a stray bullet that doesn't kill,
　　　　destruction from a failed assassination attempt,
flesh torn down the center of expectations.

Mountain

She stands on the craggy edge of granite rock
and gazes out over the hazy blue/green/purple
vista around her. This is before digital,
before everyone had cameras in their pockets,
even before phones had left the stability of walls.

She makes a mental note of the shapes
of fir and spruce trees and the way the colors
change as the space between them, full of water
and (is it?) smog, lengthens. She uses an imaginary brush
to make what is some unknown hawk into an eagle
and records it that way so that it will become majestic
and fitting of the summit of her hike that, now that I think about it,
was probably not much of a hike at all.
A few steps from the car, a young woman stands
tall and genuinely happy looking out over a clear day
in North Carolina. Maybe it really was an eagle.
It is hard to know anything for certain.

August

I know
if I had lived in 1861
I would have fought in butternut, not blue
and never known I'd sinned.
Nat Turner skinned
for doing what I like to think I'd do
if I were him.

~Andrew Hudgins, "The Unpromised Land, Montgomery, Alabama"

Before Explained From After

Her belly flattens on cement,
no growing thing opens a beat inside her.
She drums fists in a wild pattern of down strokes
like a tantrum that waited thirty years to unravel.
So she pounds until her pinky-finger knuckles
open to the bones, open to the world, to dump
rhythm into the aggregate locked inside binder.

She holds other things tightly,
listening for the thumping of heartbeats to echo:
that moment before the world called her out,
the movement of two women locked together
in saline: place before explained from after.
It breaks like flesh of a finger, pours yearning
into the crevices like red dye #40 seeping.

Her belly flattens on cement,
she sucks it in tightly to lift it up.

caverns

i scoop seeds of a cantaloupe
with a soup spoon, dropping each ball
into the sink until the orange mass
covers the drain.
switching on the disposal, i
watch the potential plants
being sucked away into a sewer system
where no soil will ever nurture them.
the expectant house looms over me like
carlsbad
where an eight-year-old me watched
the growing mud bulge and balloon
under years of single drops
of earth and stone, blood and bone
of our planet. to spice up the browns
and whites for kids like me,
the national park system set up spotlights
of reds, blues, purples, and golds
to make the stalagmites and stalactites
pulse.
i fill my flat belly, a testament to hours
of pilates and yoga, with fruit:
no stretch marks, no sagging breasts. inside,
no cell has ever grown, no replication, not
even a mistake that i could scrape away
like the scores of women i have known:
crying, conflicted, contrite
as a doctor swept away the mishaps
of youth: fertilization that came too early.
upstairs
bedrooms without beds wait for me
to make decisions, ask me how many more
years i will watch the droplets form
and then wipe them away. an echo
repeats the question, bounces between
the flat walls and the angular wedge cuts.
nothing swells, nothing grows, even the echoes
flatten.

Arkonachee Speaks

My dead mouth never produced a word,
but Arkonachee talked in a cool easy rhythm:
>   *Oh jeb wadee um fin o graka,*
>   *Seeth um granta, um jaway, uf pothem.*
She sat on the iced-over corner steps
of a run-down shop on Maple and 10th.
She propped her back against steady rows
of bricks, faced the growing street congestion,
and smiled to factory workers as we walked by.

She talked in what the girls called *Arkonachee,*
a name mixed from sounds they heard on television,
similar to the name of a tightrope walker
they adored from last year's traveling circus,
a mix that sounded native and strange.
From the name of the language, they named her.

My useless tongue could not respond, so I
smiled with a nod as she spread her blessings
in my direction. Arkonachee's arms opened
a magnificent circle before her;
she tilted her head to the right
and looked into her empty cradle.
I knew that her words comforted that imagined child
because they comforted me; I knew a cackle
could hold that nagging pain in check;
I knew because I knew empty cradles.
>   *Oh jeb wadee um fin o graka,*
>   *Seeth um granta, um jaway, uf pothem.*

As the day passed, as her blessing spread,
from deep in my throat, I laughed.
Forgetting the missing tongue, I laughed.
All day I glowed back Arkonachee sounds
to other seamstresses in the factory. I danced the fabrics
through machines with my hardened fingertips.
Under the roar of machine motors, under the smoke of threads,
my foot tapped to the sounds of our treadles thudding.

Birthday Wishes

It must be meth this time,
we whisper,
and indeed your teeth are yellow,
your eyes sunken, the purple underneath
reminds me that our faces are bone
beneath the tissue.
Your conversations hold no connecting string;
I watch your children scream out to you:
their voices and their bodies hurl themselves
as if at six and three they need to remind you
    to live for them.

We say nothing. We've honed our roles
for years: wrapped ourselves
in ribboned boxes or buried our responsibility
underneath synched bags of torn-up paper.

You fumble with carseat buckles
and their bags of favors: pinwheels and sunglasses.
We watch you drive away with their lives
burning like cake candles.

Breath of Fire

The dragon myth
must stem from a drawn lizard:
a forked tongue
on a cave wall
dancing in firelight.
Even human lungs, though,
pump more than air.
Fire, of a sort, rises
from the base of the spine,
curls itself, like a serpent
climbing a pole,
around the spine
and slithers upward:
the tail planted in earth,
the head hissing in the ear.
The tongue darts,
as a flame might,
lapping up data
for survival.
If the mythical beast
appears, multi-headed
and scaled,
will the breath
reveal itself as venom
or the purifying
burning that unveils
the present
as new?

Fish Poem

If I take the fillet knife,
slice open the belly
to remove stomach,
eggs, intestine,
can we lay sweet
white meat open
over the grill
and eat?

What is passed on

I pass the broken-down fence, split-rail boards falling in erratic patterns, and a pear tree leaning at an angle like a car swerved and tried to plow it under. I approach the stained-gray house, the burnt-red door flanked by cedar trees grown over the windows and roofline and a towering maple that was a shrub when we planted it. What's left of the grass grows wild between thigh-high weeds; bags of aluminum cans, yard sale left-overs, and two broken cars bulge from the half-opened garage. A brand new navy Celica barrels down the hill behind me, and I remember a wrecked one now hidden behind the shit in that garage. The day they brought it home was like the day they brought home my baby brother, because both were clean and beautiful, and neither belonged to me. I was five when C came home, and he was ten when they bought me a car I was too young to drive. Fourteen years and 200,000 miles later, my brother rammed that same car into a stubborn tree trunk. The scent of pinesap melts into smells of dog crap and molding suitcases, and I peek into the dark garage, look over the face-printed windshield, the bumper curled into the engine that can't possibly run anymore. I imagine his hands clutching the unmoved steering wheel as alcohol numbed his fingers white with pain. Those hands looked like mine with scars: motorcycle trouble, trouble with temper and refrigerators, trouble with machines made to grind metal, not bones. His prints still show on the door handle and on the hood where I guess he looked over the car, his life like the car, looked over what our parents gave to me, he had second hand, and wrecked. I want to ask that newly-appeared vision of him what his life was like before mom and dad split him in half, before this house started its downward spiral into a collection of decaying memories she keeps to remind us of our mistakes. I want to know what relief he found in that first sip of Jack Daniels, which fate drove that Celica out of control and out of this picture that I'm painting of and for him. I look one moment longer into the memory of my first car and his last. I want to ask him what it was for him. But the silence speaks back to me, speaks back into the unasked question, speaks to my back as I walk away.

Night Stories

She told the story in a Shoney's booth;
first, she unwrapped the ace bandage,
each loop from around her wrist fell
like a cut ribbon revealing the thinness
of her bones. The top of her hand,
was a healed blister, scorched and scabbed,
in the perfect shape of a clothing iron.

He had put the hot thing down
on her hand in a fit of anger because
she didn't bring home enough tips.
She was begging for a better section,
to pick up a few extra tables, to keep
his hands and anger off her body
for a few more nights.

The police officer, months later,
would sit in the same booth
and ask questions about her
depression, about the viability
of her husband's claim: suicide.

I had one additional story:
I rode out to their trailer
the night she tried to leave him,
to be at her side when she packed a suitcase
and picked up her six year old daughter.

She did not leave with me that night;
she did not make the extra tips either.

She did not have teeth.
She could not explain the purple marks,
the scars, the occasional limps in her walk.

Her husband was not charged.
The police officer said,

This is not Hollywood. We don't have
the money to investigate every murder.
So, it became a suicide; shot to the head
with a shotgun. Her daughter, in the next
room when she did it, was left with her father.

A Mother's Nightmare

You are the tiny rabbit, grey and white,
caged in our backyard. I run to the wires
after school with a cup of pellet food for your bowl
and blades of spring grass to feed you
through the 1-inch-square openings. I watch
      mesmerized
as you lick the spinning ball of your water bottle
to fight the already-roasting Alabama afternoons.

After you've eaten, I gently cuddle
your mass in my arms, petting fur with hopes
that one day you might not struggle
      against me.

But, today, I am met by your cries:
light but guttural
screams: the *grrekkill, grrekkill*
of rodent in crisis.
At first glance, I cannot see
a problem, only the neighbor's mutt
barking and circling as you huddle
in the center of your death-row cage.
But then, I see your bones:
your furless back legs pulled through
1-inch openings in the cage's bottom:
      predator and prey
      roles unchanged by human attempts
to domesticate both, side by side.

My father comes home from work
to finish the job. And I will punish myself,
over and over again, for failing you,
for bringing you to your death.
It is only one inch; it is only one rabbit,
but the sound of that death cry
forever chases away my sleep.

Absent Wings

                    Between
the sharp blades   of my shoulders,
      each triangular   bone blunted
by ample flesh   layers of muscle,
              knots
              clench.

        Scraps of toxins
        from which I
        can no longer fly.

September

Although the world is full of suffering, it is full also of the overcoming of it.

~Helen Keller, *Optimism*

Our Contemporary Labors

I have seen dogs prepare for labor:
·dig holes, move blankets, hide under porches.
In the final hours, they turn
on us, their human friends,
and growl as if they never slept in our beds.

I have found that same feeling
now, in my early labor: I want to be left alone,
to ignore well wishers and family
calling for updates to make plans
for their own interventions.
Instead, I curl in a ball around my son
for the last hours he will reside in my body.

But this world has created a process for delivery
that denies my body. They induce, prod,
hook up monitors, and inject medicines.
We have even let in the men,
who now try to control every possible detail:
even this final moment.

So I call no one.
My body holds his body. We roll together
in our bed. He pushes his foot into my rib cage
and turns his head against my cervix.
I run my hand down my abdomen
and tell him that I'll be here for him
when this whole procedure is finished.

It will be later, in the hard hospital lights,
with machines, extended families, and smog-filled air
that I will hold him again:
outer skin to outer skin.

Chasing Julia Strudwick Tutwiler[iii]

History lives in sheetrock like smoke
from a 3 pack-a-day smoker, the yellow
peeling in the paint. Inside these walls,
friends visit for weekends, their struggles
adding to the curls in lead-based colors.
I walk outside to wonder what memories
echo in the rocks, the dirt, in the air itself.
Thick water-heavy wind wraps live oaks
like a rope, sings the harmonies to gospel
songs without words. Watermelon pink
crape myrtles sway like folds of an ante-bellum
dress, corset underneath squeezing out
breath. My toes massage earth, contemplate
what is buried there: plot that the government
office says I *own*. Herbicides, pesticides roll
into ground water every time it rains.

Back inside the history house, I attempt
to embrace the peeling, the aching that seeps
from cracks in the foundation.
                  1660 – lifetime slavery became a legal institution
1776 – American women excluded from independence
            1838-1839 – Cherokee people driven from here to Oklahoma
                          1931 – Scottsboro boys tried for rape
        2000 – Alabama removed ban on interracial marriage with 60% of votes

My timeline continues, and I drive across farmland
leaving my rich guilt behind me. At the prison, I find
fences topped with razor wire curled like a giant Slinky.
Named for a woman who fought for reform, for women's
and inmate education, this building attempts to throw me
off, haunts me in my sleep, holds in its concrete-block walls
the screams of women I might never meet. It is not Julia,
but her hopes that I reach for. I consider the trail that led
each of us here. How many institutions have failed
Suzanne? How many men clipped Amanda's unalienable
rights? When will those scales right themselves?

Camille, dressed in white, paints the bars black;
the heavy odor filling the corridors and our lungs.
Here, free labor covers the peeling paint, and she
works to keep her history at bay. A sign says:

WET PAINT
DO NOT TOUCH

I obey because that's what my past taught me
and what my pressed, expensive clothes demand.

But under our perfected exteriors, under new layers
of tacky paint, beneath the current year in politics,
a long-jagged, corrupted, raging, and polluted river
moves. Water seeps up and out.
               I yearn to
strip down, to rip apart. To swim in the river
of paint, of water, of pain. Courage.

Log Cabin Patterns, Sestina

after Ms. Nettie Young of Gee's Bend, Alabama

We gather together with our needles
and thread to quilt together the pieced fabrics:
strips from blue skirts, yellow pants, and pieces
of ruined linens. This block shapes my memories
scattered and cut, those threads become stitches
that re-invent old scraps of faded colors

into vibrant stories with reworked colors
and patterns. I sit at the east corner, my needle
moves up and down; I make sure the stitches
pull evenly as they catch three layers of fabrics.
I get lost in the rhythm of my hand; memories
stir to consciousness: my niece's dress, pieces

from my son's shirts, husband's jeans, and pieces
from mother's tablecloth. Her favorite colors
were red and purple, and a red strip pulls memories
from me like white thread following a needle:
short waves I hardly need to watch. Her fabrics
came hard, and she tailored with extra stitches

to protect them, to make them last, stitches
to protect and bind. These purple pieces
are her songs, her radiant old fabrics
dance across like her voice. Colors
impress the women, entice them to needle
the cloth carefully, protect and bind memories

for me, for all of us, because our memories,
our strips of past reformed by stitches,
are what we hold tightly after needles
disappear, when family sleeps and pieces
blur into dreams, past the hours when colors
hold power, when all we have left is the fabric

smooth and rough between our fingers, fabrics
pulled together to keep us warm, to keep memories
boxed into rhythmic patterns with strips of colors
that were once shirts or napkins. I ripped out stitches
of dresses when I came up short and made pieces
big enough to form the log cabin blocks. Our needles

know, and they dance and sing; our needles pull together fabrics like random pieces of our lives that make stories from memories; our short and even stitches recreate from worn out colors.

Unload

for Charles

the dishwasher,
and every plate is
a metaphor: I remember
which sink in which town
gave me that chip or crack;
the tiny glass cup from my great aunt
given before she died
when she was cleaning out her cabinets,
a perfect size for dipping sauces;
pasta bowls from your sister
that are an easy shape
for black beans with cheese;
forks we stood in the aisles
and compared with every other boxed set.
We never use the silver
from our wedding gifts.

I admire the cups that have
made all fourteen of our moves
with us, the ones we used in college
before we were too snooty
for Tupperware and all things plastic,
and I stack those right beside
the new metal bottles that make us
feel somehow earth-friendly.

When I put away the cake pan,
the one I found for your birthday cake,
I place it more gently than needed
for a metal frame. It has held,
after all, the silly sugar
metaphors of one person's attempt
to please another.

Charleston, June 2015

I look across the table to my kid
whose skin is a different color from my white skin,
and I try to figure out how to tell her
what happened last night
when a white man went into a church
and shot down nine African-American people
because they were black.
How do I explain to her
that some white people are still mad
because they don't own black people anymore
that some white people are still mad
that we have to try to live up to words
like "All Men Are Created Equal"
that some white people are still mad
she could be part of my family
even though she looks different from me?
How?

But I have to try to explain it to her
when some get the luxury of turning off the television
to protect their children from those images and horrors
because she has to live in her own country
with people who are still mad
that the Japanese bombed Pearl Harbor
with people who are still mad
that they did not win in Vietnam
with men who are still mad
and want an Asian girl to boss around
to make them feel powerful and strong.

I have to teach her to protect herself.

But beside her is a little boy who looks just like me
and I have to tell him too.
I have to tell him because
white men are still thought to be trustworthy
white men are still in most positions of power

white men are still killing people when they feel sad.
And if we are ever going to change this,
It is the white boys who must be raised differently:
so that they don't go into churches and kill people.

Playing Gender

I.

> *Lying is done with words, and also with silence.*
> —Adrienne Rich, "Women and Honor: Some Notes on Lying"

I begin with I, with I
     no she no he, with I
I begin this poem there: in the space, in the silence,
     the beginning rests in the space
     the space in this poem begins
with I, where I begin.
In the space, in the silence, I open
     my mouth
I open and speak, I open
and turn to the past, to the future, I open
I turn, I speak, I begin this poem,
open my mouth and speak
     in the opening, the beginning,
tongue curls, throat vibrates,
the I speaks
     no he no she
I begin with sounds, then words.

II.

> *The collaborative space is larger and more fertile for me than writing alone.*
> —Mei-mei Berssenbrugge "By Correspondence"

You, not he not she, you listener
open your mouth to answer, you begin
our dialogue from gray, from pause,
from you.
You speak in time in time in time in,
and I from space listen
to your enunciation echo
from ripples where lines crinkle
into syllables, you fill the clock beats
with crinkled space with tonal shifts

with refusal of silence
and you speak your part
in the conversation with eloquence

you speak
no he
no she

III.

Walls around history and you
and I between walls
and history jumps between
us as we talk and history
hangs in those walls and
we talk without walls
inside history and a he flies
by on a bicycle on a raft
between walls a she flies by
in an airplane in a kite
and I am between
walls and you are between
walls and I pretend to speak
and he on the bike says you sound
like her.
You look at me you
look across the space time movement
of words you look at me
ask who he is
you ask how puppets look
between walls

IV.

In front, in the poem,
on the stage, I am she. She She She
On the stage   she talks about
houses and hair and water and fertile soil
and goddess and mothers and children
and food and style and bras and menstruation
and moon and love and love and pain
As she I   struggle
with the missing link between mean and say
the inability to   capture language.

And then, I am he. He traveling down
I-10 to the junction of entropy and villanelle
to the pinpointed logistic experiment
a tangled mass of rebar and concrete
that masquerades as a footing
deep below the bedrock of a collapsed
building.

I, now he now she, return to I
to the beginning of I where no performance
exists, return to silence
where no performance speaks
and the silence performs.

V.

We lie in silence
performing;
we write history
in our skins, in walls,
in he (that can be)
in she (that can be)

you's and I's
open and turn

Where I'm from

after Willie Perdomo

Because he nearly let his infant girl die,
left her alone in a shiny polished crib
to drive with a blaze of speed and Xanax
on a warm March night, because this story
revisits when I close my eyes,
everyone asks
where I'm from.

If I tell you that our house is falling
in on itself, grey boards bowing, bowing
under pressure of forty-year layers:
humidity and rain that just won't let up;

If I tell you that in the house's garage
a crashed Toyota Celica sits, collects dust,
hides under beer cans and spider webs
that have no other place to live;

Would you know where I'm from?

Or do I need to tell you that that house
faces west on Sunnyvale Lane,
that grass is overrun by ravenous weeds
and that salt air from the Gulf of Mexico
makes every metal bar and cup rust
into crackled sharp shards I can't forget?

Or do I need to explore inside, recover
the past by peeling up lined cupboards:
yellow flowered shelf-paper, grime
layers thicker than my lifetime, smell
of dogshit no Clorox can kill?

Where I'm from is a place lost in moss
on a house falling in on itself;
I stand on corners of pavement wondering

what ever happened to Tonka trucks
and fuchsia hoola hoops, wondering
if orange Tupperware bowls still seal
with a burp, or if the glass top table
still misses the corner, another broken
evidence of another drunk fist.

Where I'm from, though gagged and shattered,
air moves through a blooming magnolia tree,
carries a smell too sweet to enjoy.
Where ever I go, where ever I find myself,
it is that smell that I run from.

Prose Poem for Alabama

We grew up climbing trees wrapped in flowering vines of an Alabama childhood and loved battle-worn vegetation. Before waffle-bottom shoes, my sneakers would slip and slide down trunks and vines like pucks on ice, shaving away layers of skin from the tree and my legs. MaryEtta moved to Florida and I to Texas: places where trees don't have arms to hold us when our soaring flights crash. I'll never forget my initial return home, the awe of first breath laden with those forgotten smells. Now the methodical years of wisteria-bloom-buildup turns sour in my nostrils, and the odor haunts my cautious footsteps through every child-filled neighborhood. Vines may seem to meander, but real Southerners know better: every season tightens the grip, strangling the oaks in favor of false grape bunches, and releases a shower of pollen-filled petals that float on wind currents like snow flakes. My stomach overturns an urge to pick one to take home. Bees swarm; their furious furry bodies dripping with rainwater and yellow dust. Underneath suffocating shade, a dead squirrel buzzes with iridescent-green flies. Sex and death: one becoming the other. Both hum like distant airplane engines taking off somewhere, far away from red clay roads, moving life-giving liquids from one place to another. Both are here, as I walk this paved street: stooped vines touch the same road that cradles the fuzzy squirrel. I'm too early for magnolias, thick and sweet like butter and cane, and honeysuckle, delicate single drops of nectar. I settle for elephant-sized, pink azaleas and kudzu climbing the top of ogre-power poles. Substitutions become commonplace. She died less than one week ago, and I was not there. I let the flowers bring the scent of her dead body to me. I kiss it goodbye. We cannot remember the dead fondly when we see them in the hides of flattened-boney critters that only made it half way across the pavement. The dead must be honored with the fertilizing of seed, the feeding of a coming child. To drive away the absolute zero of death, we fuck by candlelight. In homespun vases, flowers erupt.

We either fight to get there
or fight to forget it.

Notes

i *Ningyou* means doll in Japanese.

ii This is the inscription chosen by Ted Hughes for the gravestone of Sylvia Plath.

iii Julia S. Tutwiler (1841-1916) was an advocate for education and prison reform in the state of Alabama. The maximum-security women's prison in Wetumpka, Alabama carries her name.

Katherine D. Perry was born in Mobile, Alabama on Christmas Eve, which aptly makes her Capricorn: both goat and fish. She grew up in nearby Spanish Fort where she learned to love fast-moving vehicles, tent camping, white-sand beaches, and the people most of the world counts out.

She discovered poetry in elementary school after writing childhood versions of magical realism stories. In poetry, she found ways to express her wild imagination without having to find a plot ending that made the package too tidy or optimistic, and she could indulge her love of sound and music. She filled notebooks with trite and rhyming metaphors about growing up in a racist and sexist world and slid them between her mattresses so that no one would ask her to explain what they meant. It wasn't until high school that she took a creative writing class and shared her poetry with other people. Perhaps not all poets are introverts, but Katherine fits the stereotype. After too-many years of undergraduate classes, she majored in English in spite of everyone's questions about what she would do with her life. She published her first poems in her student literary magazine, graduated, and moved into graduate school.

While working on her Ph.D. in American women's poetry at Auburn University, she began working with the Alabama Prison Arts + Education Project for which she taught poetry and reading classes. These classes shaped her understanding of the transformative nature of art and poetry, and they ignited in her a motivation to combine her privileged academic work with activism. She is now a tenured associate professor of English, and she is one of the founding coordinators of the Georgia State University Prison Education Project. Teaching both in a community college and in state and federal prisons, she believes that arts and education have the power to change, heal, and inspire students from all backgrounds.

Depending on point of view, fifty years can either be a long or a short time. Still, with that particular birthday on the horizon, Katherine has lately been evaluating what we are capable of doing in a single lifetime. She finds the summation of a life in a single page to be difficult, especially a life that is only half completed. But, if you were able to meet her in a bar, under dim lights and a few beverages, she might tell you: she loves to walk silently in the mountains and to commune with the trees in the tradition of what the Japanese call shinrin-yoku (forest bathing); she is committed to a yoga practice and to the Girl Scout motto: always be prepared. She adores William Faulkner's and Toni Morrison's sentences and insights. She has made more mistakes than triumphs, but she believes mistakes to be the most important and most beautiful parts of human evolution. This book is a collection of the dizzying crashes between a search for beauty and a will to acknowledge the difficulties of the human journey. Most of all, she hopes that you will find something here that inspires you to help us all to move forward. Be persistent, but swim on.